The Journey of a Lifetime

Moving to Hawaii

Dr. Diane Piela

RFW Publications—Hemet, CA

Copyright:

2019 © Diane Piela

All rights reserved. You may not reproduce any part of this book in any form or by any mechanical means including information storage and retrieval systems without written permission from the publisher, except by a reviewer, who may quote brief passages in a review.

ISBN: 978-0-9985952-4-5

Published by:

RFW Publications—Hemet, CA 92545

To those who have supported me in all of my dreams: Leslie, and my Mom and Dad.

Acknowledgements

This book would not have been possible without the support and encouragement of Leslie, as well as my mom and dad. Leslie, thank you for all the technical knowledge that you shared with me.

I extend my heartfelt and enduring thanks to those people who have guided and supported me in writing this book. Of utmost importance is my mentor and coach, Randy Powell. As an author, he was able to share his knowledge and what he learned on his journey so readily with me. Thank you for believing every person has at least one book to write and share with the world.

I wish to express my gratitude to the Island of Hawaii, and to her people, who so graciously contributed to the creation of this book with much Aloha! For without these people, there would be no book. An especially sincere "mahalo" to the West Hawaii Civic Center and its employees of the County of Hawaii, including Information Resources, Department of Motor Vehicles, Vehicle Registration and Licensing, Real Property Tax, Office of Aging, and the creators of the Hawaii County Data Book.

I also extend my gratitude for the businesses in Hawaii who gave me information and quotes for their services, which were vital to the book.

I want to express my gratitude to my editor, Paisley, for her expertise and time in polishing my manuscript. Lastly, I extend my gratefulness to my publisher

Table of Contents

Chapter 1	WHY HAWAII?	1
Chapter 2	WHICH ISLAND?	3
	Oahu, "The Gathering Place"	4
	Maui, "The Valley Isle"	8
	Hawaii, "The Big Island," or "The Orchid Isle"	12
	Kauai, "The Garden Isle"	18
Chapter 3	WHAT TO BRING?	23
Chapter 4	PREPARING TO MOVE	27
	Moving a Vehicle	35
Chapter 5	MOVING DAY	37
Chapter 6	IF YOU HAVE A PET	43
	The Five-Day-or-Less Program	46
	Exemptions	49
Chapter 7	ARRIVAL	51
Chapter 8	WHERE WILL YOU RESIDE?	55
Chapter 9	HOME OWNERSHIP & TAX BENEFITS	61
Chapter 10	CHANGE OF ADDRESS	65
Chapter 11	DRIVER'S LICENSE & REGISTRATION	69

Obtaining a Hawaii Driver's License 70
Vehicle Registration and Safety Inspection 72
    Certified Weigh Station locations: 75
    County of Hawaii DMV locations: 76

Chapter 12 ENJOY! 79

Preface

Aloha! The objective of this book is to aid the malihinis (new comers) and kama'ainas (locals, but those new to the Big Island of Hawaii) in their move to Hawaii. Perhaps you have thought about it for years, and the right opportunity has finally come along to make good on your dream? A dream you have been searching for your entire life…a dream you have held on to, but have had no idea what is involved in moving to Hawaii or how to actually do it?

Allow me to share with you my lifetime dream, my journey of a lifetime. Just before graduating from NYCOM (New York College of Osteopathic Medicine), with my Doctor of Osteopathic Medicine degree, or D.O., in 1984, I found myself with a month off from my hospital clerkships. I used this time to prepare myself for becoming a medical intern at Michigan Osteopathic Medical Center in Detroit, Michigan. My partner and friend, Leslie, treated me to a ten-day vacation in Hawaii. For both of us, it was our first time in Hawaii. We toured the islands of Oahu, Maui, and Hawaii, the Big Island. We loved it, and being young and idealistic, we thought it would be great to move to the islands one day.

I completed my internship in Detroit, then completed my three-year Family Medicine Residency in Long Island, New York in 1988. While in residency, I searched for out-of-state places to complete a one-month elective in my third year. This was partly due to my love of travelling, and not really knowing where I would end up working when I was done with my training. I found a job opportunity on the small island of Lanai, The Pineapple Island, to complete a one-month elective working under one doctor—the only doctor on the island of about 3000 residents. In order to do this, I needed to get my medical license in Hawaii, which I added to my Michigan and New York licenses. I jumped at the chance, and spent August, 1987 providing mostly office-based primary care, but also for hospitalizations and in nursing homes. I loved the people, the culture, and the island. At that time, Dole Pineapple owned most of the island where most of the residents worked.

After my month, I returned to Long Island to finish my residency. I chose to join a Family Medicine Practice in Rochester, New York, where I had grown up. As years went by, my dream was always to move West, and eventually to Hawaii.

The plan was to move out of New York State between my 50s and 60s. In between, I visited Kauai in 1997. As fate would have it, I was diagnosed with Multiple Sclerosis in 2000, and was initially out of work for four months because of severe weakness of my left hand, arm, and leg. I eventually returned part-time, and then full-time. I always had, and still have, some deficits. Over the next few years, other medical and neuro-surgical problems surfaced. Finally, I was placed on total permanent disability in 2004.

I knew living in Rochester, New York was no longer a viable option, because it was physically too difficult to deal with the snow and ice. In 2004, Leslie and I visited Molokai. Just as Kauai was a little too remote for us to live, so was Molokai. In 2004, we took a month to search out which island we would really consider moving to. Which island would be best for us to live on? We spent time renting a home on the north and east shores of Oahu. We spent time renting a condo on the island of Hawaii (Kona). We decided on the Big Island of Hawaii. Why?

From now on, when I use the name Hawaii, I will mean the Big Island. Hawaii is the biggest island by land mass, but not by population. We liked the varied climate on the island, which ranged from mountains and pasturelands, to rainforest, to semi-arid, to desert. We looked at vacation rentals, homes, and condos. We decided on a new condo complex, Na Hale O Keauhou in Kona. In fact, none of the units were even built yet.

At this time (2004-2005), we decided to sell our Spencerport, New York home and move to Southern California and Hawaii. Southern California because Leslie accepted a job as Chairperson of the American Sign Language Department at Mount San Jacinto Community College in 2005. As luck would have it, our condo in Hawaii was finished and we closed on it in March 2006. Our plan was to eventually move to Hawaii full-time.

Moving to California first gave us some time to move West but not all the way to Hawaii. We initially rented in Southern California. Then, in January 2007, we closed on a new home in Menifee, California. Moving from New York State to Hawaii full-time is a big move, one that I wasn't quite ready for yet.

After Leslie retired in 2016 and we were financially in a good position, we decided it was time to take the BIG STEP: sell our California home and move into our condo in Hawaii full-time in 2018. Guess what? We did it!

You can too! If this is truly what you want, moving to and living in Hawaii is attainable. It takes some planning, and some time and money, but it can be done. You will meet the "nay-sayers" no matter what your dream is, but I say, you can achieve your dream, if you really want it! I am writing this book because, even though there were some books about living and moving to Hawaii, I wanted to update and share my learning by experience! That's what we did! I want to share with you what worked for us, and what didn't.

What's the best way to move to Hawaii? What are your choices? How do you get there? How do you choose which island to live on? How do you choose where to live or work on that island? What to do once you are there? These questions and others are answered in the 2019 edition of *The Journey of a Lifetime: Moving to Hawaii*.

Chapter 1

WHY HAWAII?

Why move to Hawaii? The answer is: *why not?* You have the option to move anywhere you want. Let's face it, IF you have the courage, the determination, and learn "the how-to," anything is possible. If you really want to accomplish something in life…you can! It may take more time, more money, and mean more work you need to do, but you CAN move to and live in Hawaii.

There are always the "nay-sayers." They want to attach doubts to your dream. They say things like: "Don't you know how expensive it is there?"; "Don't you know Hawaii has volcanoes?"; "Don't you know

Hawaii has hurricanes?"; "Don't you know Hawaii has sharks?"; "Hawaii is for vacations, not to live there." The questions and comments go on and on...

If you look up the healthiest and best state to live in, Hawaii is ranked #1. It is number one for access and affordability of healthcare, too. It has the third-lowest adult obesity rate in the nation. This is all based on 2018 data. Hawaii's total population is 1.4 million. The Median Household Income is $70,531 (the average for all states is $62,470). The population below the Federal Poverty Level is 22 percent (Radley, McCarthy, & Hayes, 2018) (the average of all states is 32 percent).

I will share other statistics with you, such as taxes, cost of living, etc., later in this book.

You have your own reasons and really don't need to explain them to anyone. Follow your dream.

Chapter 2

WHICH ISLAND?

Just because you say that you want to move to Hawaii, that doesn't mean you know *which* island, or what part of that island you want to live on. The Hawaiian Islands are an archipelago, a group or chain of islands. The state of Hawaii recognizes up to 137 islands, though most are uninhabited. The eight major islands are Oahu, Hawaii, Maui, Kauai, Lanai, Molokai, Kahoolawe, and Niihau. No two Hawaiian Islands are alike, and each has their own vibe. I have been to six of the eight major islands, and I know Oahu and Hawaii the best. I will touch on Oahu, Maui, Hawaii, and Kauai, the four most populated islands. I should start out by saying that, if you are in a position to choose which island you live on (retirement, home business, disabled, not working), I recommend spending time on each island, at least two to four weeks on each of the islands you are seriously considering. Also, visiting multiple times gives you better knowledge of the islands. Visit in different seasons. This way, you'll really get the feel of the island, especially outside of the hotel areas. This is a great time to use VRBO, HomeAway, etc. to rent a home. Obviously, if you are in the military and get orders or have accepted a job, or are accepted by one of the colleges, you don't choose the island, but you do choose *where* on that island to live.

Oahu, "The Gathering Place"

When some people think of Hawaii, Oahu is what they think of. Oahu is the third-largest island and is forty-four miles long and thirty miles wide. Oahu is the busiest, most populated island in the state of Hawaii. The population estimate as of 2018 is 988,650 ("Quick Facts: Honolulu County," U.S. Census Bureau, 2018).

Most of Hawaii's 1.4 million people live here ("Quick Facts :Hawaii County and State of Hawaii", 2018.). It is, without a doubt, the easiest of the islands to find work and go to school on. If you want nationally known restaurants and nightlife, then Oahu is for you. Oahu has more jobs, more roads, more traffic, more shopping, more tourists, and more things to do than any of the other islands. The University of

Chapter 2

Hawaii has three campuses, two of which are on Oahu-Manoa and West Oahu, plus seven community colleges scattered throughout the islands.

There is no doubt that your choices for medical care are vast on Oahu. Seven major medical facilities and full-service hospitals are available in Honolulu alone: The Queen's Medical Center; Straub Medical Center; Kaiser Permanente Moanalua Medical Center; Tripler Medical Center; Kapi'olani Medical Center for Women and Children; Shriner's Hospital; and Kuakini Medical Center.

On other parts of Oahu, there are: Adventist Health Castle (Kailua); Hawaii State Hospital (Kaneohe); Kahuku Medical Center (Kahuku); Pali Momi Medical Center (Aiea); and Wahiawa General Hospital (Wahiawa). There is also a Veteran's Administration Medical Center, and many other medical clinics and health centers throughout Oahu.

Hawaii is headquarters for the U.S. Pacific Command and all five branches of the service are represented here. There are approximately 100,000+ military personnel and dependents across the Hawaiian Islands, with the largest number represented on Oahu. The military bases impact civilians as well, and have created 100,000+ civilian jobs, too. In all, there are more choices of services and housing on Oahu.

Honolulu lives up to its name as the capital city of Hawaii, and as the seat of government on Oahu. It is the principle port, major airport, tourism, business, financial, and educational center of the state. Yet, with all the diversity on Oahu, there are poorer areas of Oahu, as well as wealthy suburbs, surf towns, and farmlands in Wahiawa. As for the landscape, there are the two extinct shield volcanoes' mountain ranges, the Waianae and Koolau, and many beaches. Oahu also has historical areas, such as Pearl Harbor and the Pacific Aviation Museum, with the USS Missouri Naval Ship, and the ultimate center of Hawaiian history and cultural museums, Iolani Palace, Queen Emma's Summer Palace, and Bishop Museum.

With almost a million residents, traffic conditions are challenging. The bulk of the workforce is either heading to a military base or into town. Normal weekday rush hour is 5 a.m. to 8 a.m. going inbound to Honolulu, and 3 p.m. to 6:30 p.m. going outbound. Expect heavy traffic on Interstates H-1 and H-2, and on Nimitz Highway/Ala Moana Boulevard. During off-peak hours, it may take you ten minutes to drive from Waikiki to Pearl Harbor. During rush hour, it can be a minimum of thirty minutes.

Keep in mind that Oahu, like the other islands, has a very diverse feel, not only on an emotional level but also a physical level, namely the people, environment, scenery, and weather. For example, it might be hot and sunny on the "Leeward" (West) side and raining and windy on the "Windward" (East) side of an island at the same time.

Chapter 2

Living on the North Shore (NS), there are communities such as Haleiwa, Laie, and Hauula that are legendary surf towns. They still have a vibe of being laid-back towns, but the country feel and land with privacy come at a price.

Living on the Leeward (West) side of Oahu, such as Kapolei, Ewa Beach (population 14,955) ("Quick Facts: Honolulu County," U.S. Census Bureau, 2018), and Ko'olina, these areas have seen an explosion of construction, both residential and commercial. There is a large military population here. It is a more suburban feel, with newer and larger homes for families.

Living on the Windward (East) side, you pass over lush green mountains on H-61 or the Pali Highway. Coming out of the tunnels on the Pali, you will marvel at the beauty. This side of the island, with towns such as Hawaii Kai, Kaneohe (population 34,597) ("Quick Facts: Honolulu County," U.S. Census Bureau, 2018), and Kailua, has some of the highest priced real estate, but the hiking trails and calm waves of the beaches are expansive.

Waianae (population 13,177) ("Quick Facts: Honolulu County," U.S. Census Bureau, 2018) and Wahiawa (population 17,821) ("Quick Facts: Honolulu County," U.S. Census Bureau, 2018) warrant mention. Wahiawa is the Central Valley between the Waianae and Koolau Mountains. The median income is lower here, with higher unemployment and a higher crime rate. If you are moving from the Mainland, the old saying still holds for many: stay away from the Ws.

You will need to investigate for yourself what areas are better for you and your family. There is an advantage to renting, because you can always move when your rental contract is up.

A little bit about affordability on Oahu, Maui, The Big Island, and Kauai. I will go over this more later, but Oahu ranks as the highest for housing costs, followed by Maui, Kauai, and Hawaii. Utilities follow the same pattern. To offset this, Oahu's salaries are generally higher than the other islands, and jobs are more competitive.

Maui, "The Valley Isle"

Maui is the second-largest island, with a width of twenty-six miles and a length of forty-eight miles. The estimated population from 2018 was 166,348 ("Quick Facts: Maui County" US Census Bureau, 2018).

It has miles and miles of beautiful beaches. Most of the population lives in the central or southern areas. Jobs on Maui are primarily in tourism, construction, agriculture, education, medicine, and technology, or are entrepreneurial.

The main areas to live in are Wailuku (Central Maui), Haleakala, Northeast Maui, or South, East, or West Maui.

Central Maui

Chapter 2

Wailuku is just south of Kahului (airport). It is the third-largest town on Maui, with a population of 15,313 ("Quick Facts: Maui County" US Census Bureau, 2018). It is now overshadowed by the resort town of Ka'anapali. It is the main populated area where the airport, malls, ports for shipping and receiving, and many local businesses can be found. It is the seat of the Maui County Government, and at the mouth of the Iao Valley.

The major employers include Maui Memorial Medical Center, Kaiser Permanente, Maui County, and the correctional facility.

Maui has had an explosion of people and houses over the past twenty years. The nearest university is the University of Hawaii Maui College in Kahului (two miles away).

Kahului is the largest, most populated town on Maui, with a population of 26,337. It is extremely close to the best amenities for living: banks, big shopping, groceries, Costco, libraries, restaurants, movies, and venues for events. It is also close for driving to the North Shore and Up Country. Kahului is where the main airport is. It is very commercial. The one thing it isn't close to is all the nice beaches.

West Maui

Ka'anapali is primarily a tourist town, full of beaches. It started with development in the 1960s as a resort a few miles north of Lahaina (old whaling town). Since then, many hotels and condos have been built, and have turned Lahaina from a quaint town to a tourist shopping area and harbor for excursions.

Lahaina was once the capital of the Hawaiian Kingdom, a historic whaling village in the mid-1800s. Its estimated population is 11,704 ("Quick Facts: Maui County" US Census Bureau, 2018).

It has been transformed into a hotspot for art galleries, unique shops, and restaurants. Its harbor is a takeoff for many whale-watching, snorkel, scuba, and boat excursions. Between Maui and The Big Island of Hawaii are found many humpback whales, as this is their breeding, mating, and birthing ground due to the warm, shallower waters between November and April annually. Then they swim up to California and Alaska for the rest of the year to feed. This area is part of a National Whale Sanctuary. It was created by Congress in 1992 to protect the endangered humpback whales. The sanctuary is located off the coasts of the four islands: Maui, the north and south shores of Oahu, the north shore of Kauai, and the Kohala and Kona coasts of Hawaii.

Upcountry Maui (Pukalani, Olinda, and Kula)

Haleakala is a ten thousand-foot inactive volcano that towers over the island. Makawao is a small village on the way up to Haleakala, where countryside living takes place. This is an agricultural area for Maui's onions. Cooler temperatures with high-elevation views are found here. Maui's oldest and largest family-owned cattle ranch, since the 1880s and

Chapter 2

with more than thirty thousand acres, is found here. This area is really far from the beaches, because there is no direct road from Kula to Kihei.

Northeast Maui

Northeast Maui is beautiful to vacation in and is known for its Road to Hana, and Hana itself. It is far from everything, but mainly stores and restaurants. Hana is an escape more than a place to live.

South Maui

Wailea is fifteen hundred acres of luxurious beaches, resorts, and attractions. If you don't mind some crowds and a resort vibe, this is the place for you. It seems the budget-conscious people end up in Kihei and the luxury-seeking people in Wailea.

Kihei has a population of 20,881 ("Quick Facts: Maui County" US Census Bureau, 2018). Several research facilities are located here, including seed operations by DeKalb, Monsanto, and the Maui Research Technology Park. Many Southern Californians have transplanted here for technological jobs.

Finding a place to live on Maui can be one of the hardest parts about moving to Maui. It is best to find a place to rent once you are on the island. Then, you are taken seriously and can check Craigslist or work with a realtor.

I will comment about traffic. It is hard to judge how long it will take you to get somewhere. As an example, if you live Upcountry but work on the West Coast, there will be traffic. You may be only twelve miles away from work, but if you are driving a mountain road and driving through a business or tourist area, you can't just say it will take twenty minutes. Twelve miles straight across Maui isn't necessarily twelve miles by road access.

There are three hospitals on Maui. Maui Memorial Hospital is the only acute hospital on Maui and is in Wailuku, approximately four miles from the airport.

Kula Hospital is a critical access hospital located in the southern part of Maui, in Kula. The Cancer Institute of Maui is in Wailuku. Hana Medical Center works in cooperation with American Medical Response and Maui Memorial Medical Center.

Hawaii, "The Big Island," or "The Orchid Isle"

The Big Island, as it's named, is the largest island of the Hawaiian Archipelago in the Pacific. It is the most southeastern of the chain of Hawaiian Islands. It is also the most southern point, South Point (Ka Laae), of all the United States. Hawaii is ninety-three miles long and seventy-six miles wide (same size as Connecticut). However, it only has 13 percent of Hawaii's population. Hawaii County's estimated population in 2018 is 200,038 ("Quick Facts: Hawaii County" US Census Bureau, 2018). The Big Island has grown in population the most of all the islands, with an annual increase of 1.1 percent. Hawaii is more

Chapter 2

attractive to people looking to relocate because of its relatively lower cost of living, as compared to its neighboring islands, especially Oahu and Maui.

The Big Island is one of the most ecologically diverse places in the world. The island boasts eleven of thirteen climate zones in the world (or 8, 9, or 10, depending on which classification system used). Factors such as elevation, pressure variations, rainfall, wind, and topography combine to create distinctive locations throughout the island. Some of the climates that you may encounter are: humid, tropical zones; arid and semi-arid zones; the temperate zones; and the alpine zones. All the other Hawaiian Islands have four climate zones each.

West Hawaii

Kailua-Kona (plus Holualoa) is the largest town on Hawaii's West Side. Its estimated population as of 2018 is 28,850 ("Quick Facts: Hawaii County" US Census Bureau, 2018). It has a tropical, semi-arid climate with warm temperatures year-round. It is the warmest place in the US in January. Throughout the year, the average highs are 81-87 and lows are 68-75. It is generally dry, with approximately thirty-two inches of rain per year. For this reason, it is the center of commerce and tourism on West Hawaii.

Its post office is designated Kailua-Kona to differentiate it from Kailua on the Windward side of Oahu. The community was the seat of government in 1795, and later when King Kamehameha unified the kingdom of Hawaii. It later served as a retreat for the Hawaiian Royal Family. The capital was later moved to Lahaina, Maui, and finally Honolulu. In the late twentieth and twenty-first centuries, this region has undergone a real estate and construction boom fueled by tourism and investments.

Kona is currently enjoying an upward turn in economy, real estate, and investments. Tourism is increasing, and cruise ships stop in Kona at least once a week (Wednesdays).

The University of Hawaii has established its Hawaii Community College Palamanui Campus in Kona. It offers multiple programs, such as Liberal Arts, Culinary Arts, Hospitality and Tourism, Tropical Forest Ecosystem, Nursing (AS), Fire Science, and Human Services, to name a few. At the writing of this book, it has a new Civic Center and new courthouse as well.

There are five hospitals on the Big Island: The Kona Community Hospital in Keauhou; North Hawaii Community Hospital in Waimea (just north of Kona); Kohala Hospital in Kapaau (northern-most point); Ka'u Hospital (Pahala); and Hilo Medical Center in Hilo.

Northern Hawaii

Waimea, or Kamuela is the biggest town (population 12,160) ("Quick Facts: Hawaii County" US Census Bureau, 2018) on the north

Chapter 2

side of the Big Island. Since there are three Waimea's in Hawaii—Waimea in Oahu, Waimea in Kauai, and Waimea on the Big Island—Kamuela is also Waimea on the Big island. Waimea is the Hawaiian equivalent of Samuel. Samuel Parker (1853-1920) was the son of John Parker, patriarch of the Parker Family, who owns much of the land around Waimea, with 135,000 acres known as Parker Ranch, the oldest and largest privately-owned ranch in the United States.

Waimea was a company town, and still has a strong ranch atmosphere. Waimea is made out of the oldest of five volcanoes on the Big Island, the Kohala Mountains. Because Waimea is 2500+ feet up, the temperatures are cooler compared to Kona, and low clouds obscure the lush, rolling pastures. There is a dry and a wet side of Waimea, where the difference is visually obvious due to rainfall.

There are new housing divisions, and the Parker Schools have a great reputation. The big employers are tourism (big hotels in Waikoloa and golf courses), education, medicine (Hilo Med Center and North Kohala Community Hospital), and Parker Ranch.

Southern Hawaii (Oceanview, Volcano, and Na'alehu)

Southern Hawaii is raw and filled with powerful beauty. Oceanview, with an estimated population of 4,726" in 2018 ("Quick Facts: Hawaii County" US Census Bureau, 2018), is in the Ka'u district, near South Point (Kaalae). It is the most southern point of Hawaii, and of the fifty United States. Living here means living a rugged life amidst lava fields and few modern conveniences. People here are self-sufficient and don't want to be bothered; they chose a life off the grid.

There is no county water or sewer. Therefore, cesspool or septic is the rule. Water needs to be transported in, and homes usually have at least one water tank and a water pump. Although phone, electricity, and satellite capabilities are available, some homes don't have them. They use portable potties and collect rainwater (catchment system). There are two markets for groceries, which are both extremely expensive compared to Kona or Hilo. There is a post office, a veterinary office, and a few restaurants for pizza, sandwiches, and burgers. Land is cheap—just black, hard lava, and not much gets through it. Houses are cheap and can be anything from a yurt to a container, to a cabin or a three-bedroom home on one level within a gated community.

Na'alehu and Volcano are even smaller, but have some historical and tourist landmarks, such as the Monkey Pod tree planted by Mark Twain, the most southern bakery in Punalu'u, black and green sand beaches, and of course, Hawaii Volcanoes National Park. I need to mention that there are two volcanoes in this area, Mauna Loa and the very active Kilauea. Mauna Loa last erupted in 1984, and Kilauea erupted from January 1983 through the recent May 2018 eruption. The large

Chapter 2

eruption that began in May 2018 and ended September 2018 destroyed 700 homes.

East Hawaii

Hilo is the center of East Hawaii and is the county seat of government and largest town, with an estimated population of 45,579 people in 2018 ("Quick Facts: Hawaii County" US Census Bureau, 2018). Hilo is a quaint town with some very old buildings—still being used, I may add.

Employment on the Big Island is made up of small businesses, which make up 60 percent of the work force. Tourism employs 17 percent. Then agriculture, namely coffee, macadamia nuts, and orchids. The remaining employment is provided by government, medicine, and education; Hilo houses the University of Hawaii Hilo campus.

Astronomy is also an important industry on the island. Mauna Kea is the tallest mountain (volcano) of the Pacific, and it hosts the world's largest astronomical observatory, and thirteen telescopes representing eleven countries.

Hilo usually has somewhat cooler temperatures than Kona but is also more humid, with Hilo averaging almost 130 inches of rain annually. It rains an average of 272 days throughout the year in Hilo.

The Journey of a Lifetime Moving to Hawaii

Kauai, "The Garden Isle"

Kauai is the most northern and western of the major Hawaiian Islands. It is the fourth largest of the Hawaiian Islands. The island averages twenty-six miles in diameter. At its longest point, it is thirty-three miles, and twenty-five miles at its shortest. Although Kauai has ninety miles of shoreline, it has more beaches per mile than any other Hawaiian Island. The population of Kauai is estimated to be 72,159 in 2018 ("Quick Facts: Kauai County," US Census Bureau, 2018).

Just as Hawaii is the youngest of the Hawaiian Isles, Kauai is the oldest, formed some six million years ago. The highest peak on Kauai is Kawaikini (5,243 ft). Most of the interior is mountainous, with Mount Waialeale, the second-highest peak (5,148 ft), averaging over 480 inches of rain per year, leading it to be deemed "the wettest place on earth." All this rain cascades to form waterfalls, streams, and rivers. Waimea River is the state's longest, at twenty miles. Most of the population lives along the shores, like Lihue (population 6455), Kapa'a (population 10,699), Hanapepe, Hanalei, Poipu Beach, and Princeville ("Quick Facts: Kauai County," US Census Bureau, 2018).

Employment can be difficult on the smaller islands like Kauai; the entire island is built on tourism. Next are construction and healthcare, only after retail and sales.

Chapter 2

Kauai has three hospitals: Wilcox Memorial in Lihue, Samuel Mahelona Memorial Hospital in Kapa'a, and Kauai Veterans Memorial hospital in Waimea.

Southeast and East Kauai

Lihue is the second-largest city and is the seat of government of Kauai County. Its population is estimated at 6,455 in 2018("Quick Facts: Kauai County," US Census Bureau, 2018). With the emergence of the sugar industry in the 1800s, Lihue was the central city after the construction of a large sugar mill. However, their sugar industry shut down in 1996. They could not compete with the much less labor-intensive competitors in other countries.

The city is home to the county administration, Kauai's largest shopping center, and Kukui Grove, which houses Macy's, Walmart, Home Depot, and Costco. Lihue is also home to Kauai Community College and elementary, middle and high schools, and is served by the Lihue Airport.

Kapa'a is the city with the largest population on the island, with 10,699 residents("Quick Facts: Kauai County," US Census Bureau, 2018).

It is eight miles north of Lihue. Everything is smaller on Kauai, because Kauai itself is smaller—everything but the cost of living. To be fair, Oahu is the most expensive of the four islands to live on, followed by Kauai and Maui. The Big Island is most affordable, based on housing costs.

South Kauai

Poipu is a tourist's dream, surrounded by beautiful white sand beaches, high-end hotels, resorts, golf courses, and one main shopping center. There are also many condos, vacation rentals, and second homes that make up this area. You can assume property and homes are very expensive here. The population in the Kaloa-Poipu area is estimated to be 6,208 from 2017-2018("Quick Facts: Kauai County," US Census Bureau, 2018).

Kaloa was the home of the first successful sugar cane plantation in Hawaii in 1835.

Hanapepe's population in 2018 is estimated to be 2,876. ("Quick Facts: Kauai County," US Census Bureau, 2018) The town was the inspiration for Kokaua Town in the fictional hometown of Disney's *Lilo and Stitch*. It is also the headquarters for the ice cream company, Lappert's Hawaii.

West Kauai

Waimea is a popular town with hikers and tourists because it is the entrance to Waimea Canyon, also known as the Grand Canyon of the Pacific. The canyon is quite remarkable, considering it is on a small island. It is ten miles long and up to three thousand feet deep.

Chapter 2

It has been formed by erosion from the rain coming off the slopes of Mt. Wai'ale'ale, forming the Waimea River. It was also formed in part by the catastrophic collapse of the volcano that created Kauai.

Waimea has an estimated population of 1,870 in 2018("Quick Facts: Kauai County," US Census Bureau, 2018). Its main industries are construction and tourism.

North Kauai

The Napili Coast spans seventeen miles of Kauai's north shore, which is dominated by four thousand-foot cliffs that are accessible by air and water. The main cities on the north shore are Princeville and Hanalei. Hanalei Town is a beautiful town with Mt. Na Molokama and Mt. Mamalahoa in the back. It was the backdrop for several films produced, such as *South Pacific* (1958). Its population is under one thousand, and its primary employment is tourism.

Princeville has a population of 8,340 as of 2017-2018("Quick Facts: Kauai County," US Census Bureau, 2018). It is the northernmost and largest of the cities. Again, tourism is the primary industry.

Because Kauai is more remote and smaller, with less people, Kauai can give you a more rustic, off-the-grid life, if that is what you are looking for. However, there are some very high-priced areas on Kauai, as far as land and housing.

Chapter 3

WHAT TO BRING?

It may be said of moving in general, we bring too much from one home to another. This is especially true in moving across the country, or from the Mainland to Hawaii. Everyone I talk to about "their move" says the same thing: "We brought too much!"

It can be hard when sorting through to decide what to get rid of and what to keep when you are talking about moving to an island. A lot of things you use on the Mainland may not be necessary on an island. Hawaii living emphasizes simplicity and getting by with less.

I recommend keeping your personal things that have sentimental value first. These items are priceless, like albums, photographs, souvenirs from travelling, family heirlooms that were handed down to you, and gifts that have special meaning. Musical instruments, household items that may be hard to buy in Hawaii, historical items, collectible items, one-of-a-kind gardening tools, etc. should also be moved to Hawaii. It all depends on the person and what she/he values.

Because we owned a condo in Kona for twelve years before moving to Hawaii full time, we purchased all our furniture in Hawaii. The only furniture that we moved to Hawaii when we moved here permanently were my piano and bench, two reupholstered chairs that my dad had originally upholstered years ago, two small antique desks that have been in the family for years, a pine trunk, two antique book shelves, a rocking chair that was my retirement gift, my exercise bike, a pet grooming table, and a unique, antique dresser.

Many homes, condos for sale, and rentals come completely furnished, even down to the plates, pans, and kitchen utensils. Unless you buy new construction, as we did with our condo, Kona on the Big Island has Walmart, Target, Costco, and Macy's. Hilo on the Big Island has Costco, Walmart, Sears, and JC Penney. Oahu has four Costcos, and Maui and Kauai have one each. I bought most of my kitchen supplies in Hawaii but did ship over my mixer, glass items, heirloom or sentimental items, and my favorite hard-to-find items like my rolling pin, Christmas cookie cutters, and cake tester. Many things in our condo, I purchased

Chapter 3

through mail order or online and had them shipped to Kona (such as lamps). Look for FREE SHIPPING, because things can cost more and take more time to ship to Hawaii.

Because we moved from Upstate New York to California and then Hawaii, we got rid of all our winter clothing, for sure. We brought light jackets, sweaters, and raincoats. I have a few warmer jackets for when we go to the volcano, Mauna Kea. For the Big Island, as you go up in elevation up the volcano, night temperatures are colder, and some people use a heater or fireplace to be warm as far as in their homes. It is also cooler at night on the north, east, and south shores of the Big Island, especially in winter. We got rid of most of our fancy clothes, except a few dresses and dress shoes for being off the island, for cruises or weddings on the Mainland.

We had multiple garage sales, from a few years before to right before we moved. Alternatively, you could have an estate sale. If we didn't sell things, we donated them. Example: We had many projectors and cameras, and we donated them to a museum. We had old military uniforms from WWI, WWII, and the Vietnam War, and we donated those to a museum too. We had an appraiser come out to appraise anything we thought was valuable, before we sold it. We had a gold/silver appraiser come by to weigh and see the value of any old jewelry, military pins, etc. We sold or donated all medical antiques and books. We used eBay, Craigslist, and local online marketplace sites through Facebook to sell everything from furniture and clothing to collectibles (Lenox china, nutcrackers, Beanie Babies). All books we didn't sell, we donated to a few local libraries. Lastly, we donated to the Salvation Army, Goodwill, and the local Lions Club for their annual garage sale. We started six months before to give ourselves time. Just make sure you get a receipt or letter from whoever you donated to, to use for tax exemptions.

Remember that, if you are shipping in a container or using a moving company, shipping by boat is by the square foot and not weight. If shipping by UPS or the US Postal Service, size and weight may both be important.

Even when we cleaned out everything in advance, we thought we would have maybe sixty medium boxes of belongings to be sent…

Well, it turned into double that by the time we actually packed everything to be shipped. This brings us to the next chapter: Preparing for the Move.

Chapter 4

PREPARING TO MOVE

How do you do it? In moving from the Mainland, as the contiguous United States is referred to, to Hawaii, your choices are to: move by pod and pack and fill it yourself, or hire a moving company to pack and fill the pod; hire a moving company that specializes in moving off the Mainland, such as Royal Hawaiian Movers or Prime Movers, to take care of everything; hire a shipping company like Matson, Pasha, or Young's; or mail or UPS everything. All prices for shipping or for moving companies are based on a very simple principle: you either pay a set price for a full container or a price based on actual space or square feet.

I will first discuss the easiest and most expensive way, using a professional moving company. This certainly has its advantages. This is what we did. We packed all our stuff in boxes or bins. If you pack yourself, you MUST double-wrap everything. Don't forget your things are going in a truck, and maybe storage, before being loaded through the air and onto a cargo ship. The ship will be bounced about side by side and front to back, even without a storm. We wrapped everything breakable (glass, china, ceramic) in paper first and then bubble wrap. If you don't, expect many things to be broken. A friend packed their own container with boxes, and they loaded the boxes themselves, and almost all glass items were broken.

So, how do you find a moving company? First, find a company that specializes in Hawaiian or overseas moves. Make sure you use a company that specializes in moves between California (or other states) and Hawaii. Why? You want movers who have employees or people they work with in California AND Hawaii. Otherwise, the company may subcontract out, and you have no control over it. It should have a base of operation in California and Hawaii, or utilize a reputable agent to perform the delivery process.

Luckily for us, we were able to find a professional moving company with bases in California and Hawaii. First, we packed everything ourselves, which saved us a lot of money. Next, I searched

Chapter 4

out professional movers on the internet. I called three for quotes and asked each how their company works. The following are four examples of "how you can move."

Example 1:

We decided which three days we would likely move. The Professional Movers gave me a three-day window of when they would load everything up. You need to schedule all this in advance. Twenty-four hours before arriving, they called me to notify me of exactly when they would be at my home.

They record every box and every piece of furniture with a number. They shrink-wrap the boxes two or three boxes high for easier loading. Some boxes were wrapped in quilted moving blankets. All furniture was wrapped in the quilted pads and shrink-wrapped. They built wooden crates for every piece of furniture with glass (such as my dresser). They built a custom cardboard and padded crate for my piano. They custom wrapped all large pictures and mirrors. Then, they loaded everything in a truck and delivered it to the pier in Long Beach, California. Because they needed to wait a day until a ship going to Hawaii was available, they stored it for a day or two. Storage for up to three days was included in the price. Then, they loaded everything into a container. Most containers are twenty or forty feet. It was loaded at Long Beach Pier on a cargo ship that first went to Oahu and then the Big Island.

The Journey of a Lifetime Moving to Hawaii

Actually, November was a great time to move because it took less than two weeks to be delivered to our condo in Kona. I received an email and phone call when it arrived in Hilo. The moving company unloaded it onto a truck and called me the day before it was unloaded, then delivered some to my condo and some to storage. They inventoried every numbered box to make sure it was delivered (five of our boxes were missing). Then, I needed to report to the company and insurance verbally and in print what was damaged, pictures of what was damaged, and what was missing, with the value of each item (item, brand, age, fair market value—eBay is a good reference).

All in all, we were amazed at the care and packing they provided. I had one cover of a casserole bowl broken, and two laminated-wood, white craft files broken. After they unloaded everything, we inventoried everything to see what was damaged or missing. Five boxes were missing. The insurance for moving I purchased through the movers cost me $298 for $7000.00 worth of insured goods. I filled out forms with pictures of what was missing, value today, and brand (three of the things were brand new, in the original boxes, so I just looked up how much I paid online).

Our one fault was that we didn't itemize our dog grooming equipment, that we'd purchased only five months before. Because we didn't have it as an itemized valuable, we weren't reimbursed. We were

Chapter 4

reimbursed after all photos and paperwork for everything else were sent within sixty days from delivery, for $400 in broken or missing items. Fortunately, I also had photos I took of all the boxes in the garage waiting for loading. There was a $50 deductible, so I received $350 by check. I guess it was worth it, because I only paid $298 for the insurance. The thing is, you need to itemize all the big or expensive pieces and have an idea of what is in each box. Also, the insurance company would not insure plastic bins or used boxes. I always thought plastic bins were stronger, but I can tell you, no cardboard boxes were damaged, whereas one plastic bin was crushed (probably from stacking).

If I hadn't bought extra insurance, I believe the company said I would only be insured $0.70 per pound. So, if I had a damaged ten-pound television, I would only get $7.00 from the basic insurance provided.

I only had to pay $100 (refundable) as a deposit to reserve my place with a window of three possible moving days. Overall, we paid $8000 for loading, packing, shipping, and unloading at two addresses (storage and condo), for twelve pieces of furniture, about 120+ medium boxes, and the custom crates that were made for some furniture. They did give me a discount, as well as a discount on shipping our car. More on vehicles later.

Example 2:

The Journey of a Lifetime Moving to Hawaii

If you decide not to go with a professional moving/shipping company, another option is to ship by Matson directly. Currently, Matson only ships twenty-foot containers, which would cover about a two- to three-bedroom apartment. You would need to pack everything into boxes yourself. Call Matson at least two to three days before, so they can dispatch a truck with the container. Matson will leave the container at your home for ten days.

You need to arrange an authorized trucking company to pick up and drop off your container at the ports. This includes trucking to pick the container up at your home and transfer it to the Port of Long Beach, California. You will also need to order an authorized trucking company to pick it up at the Port of Hilo (Kawaihae, Honolulu, Kahului, or Lihue). Security is present at all the ports now. When the trucking company delivers the container to you, remember the container is four feet up from the ground, with no ramps. You will have ten days to unload it and will need to call the trucking company to pick it up in those ten days.

So, what is the cost of this? It is based on footage more than weight. The ocean freight from Long Beach, California to Oahu is $4700. The Hawaii port fees are $103. The Invasive Species check is $7.50. Then, there are port service and fuel charges. The cost of the ferry to the Big Island is another $1000. All these prices vary depending on

Chapter 4

where pick up and drop off are. Other West Coast ports are in Oakland and Seattle. Delivery ports are: Honolulu; Kahului Maui; Hilo, Hawaii; Kawaihae, Hawaii; and Nawiliwili, Kauai. The total with taxes and fees is about $5700. With trucking fees to and from a port included, the total is $6700. Again, it depends on how far you are from the ports to ship out and to deliver, and remember, this is if you pack everything in boxes yourself and load and unload yourself. You can hire a company to do it, but if you do, you may just as well have a professional mover do it all, like in the first example.

Example 3:

PODs are popular for moving. The most common POD is sixteen feet for a three-bedroom house. This compares to a ten- by fifteen-foot storage or a twenty-foot truck. There are also twelve and seven feet. POD will drop off and deliver the POD to your existing home, and they will deliver it to the port on the Big Island, but not to your new home. Actually, what happens is, POD will deliver the POD to your existing home and leave it for the time you need to load it. When loaded, you call POD to pick it up. They take it to the Long Beach Port (or another West Coast port) and from there it is transported to the ship. All the PODS go to Oahu first and are unloaded to a ferry to your port destination.

POD will deliver to Hilo or Kawaihae on the Big Island but won't deliver to your home in Hawaii. When it arrives in Hilo, you will be notified and given forty-eight hours to unload the POD by a trucking company reserved in advance or by yourself. The travel time by ship is twenty-three to thirty days. Packing and loading yourself at your existing home and unloading yourself at the port destination (within forty-eight hours), costs about $5500. Again, if you hire movers to unload it from the ship to deliver it, there is an added charge. Insurance is $49.95 per month. One nice feature of POD is, if you don't have a destination address, they will deliver it to the nearest POD Storage, but there isn't a POD Storage on the Big Island. So, you save a little doing it this way.

Example 4:

You can mail everything by USPS Priority. Maximum weight is 70 pounds in the Flat Rate Boxes:

SMALL - 8 5/8" x 5 5/8" - $7.95

MEDIUM - 11" x 8" x 5" - $ 14.35

LARGE - 12" x 12" x 6" - $ 19.95

When sending by mail to or from Hawaii, you always want to use Priority, at least, to receive your package within three to five days. Otherwise, normal mail can take a month by boat. Priority also has tracking.

Chapter 4

Of course, you are more limited by mail, but if you don't have furniture, it is something to think about. Example: If I mailed my 120 large boxes Priority, the cost would be about $2400, but not everything will fit in a large Priority box, so it would cost more than that.

Moving a Vehicle

If you have a new car or a car in good condition, we recommend shipping it over to Hawaii. Roughly, most cars cost $1000-$1500. You need to drop it off at the port of shipping and pick it up at the port of your destination. Or, you can hire someone to pick it up and drop it off. We reserved a place on a ship by paying $874 with the same professional moving company that did our other moving. I received a discount because I used the same company for both.

When you drop off the car, it has to be clean, washed inside and out, with all personal items removed. I received a reservation number, which I gave to the port office, along with my current auto registration, photo ID, and a check for full payment. When our car arrived in Hilo, I got a text and phone call that our car was ready for pick up. They would hold the car for seventy-two hours. At the Port of Hilo, we needed to show our current driver's license and photo ID. I will go into more about transferring your driver's license, obtaining your auto registration, and safety inspection in a later chapter.

The Journey of a Lifetime Moving to Hawaii

The other option is going through Matson yourself, since they are the shipping company that ships vehicles too. Call 1-800-4MATSON and press "1" for shipping rates, press "2" for shipping personal belongings, press "3" for dropping off a vehicle, and press "4" for picking up a vehicle. The average cost to ship a vehicle from Long Beach to Hawaii is $1070. The average price for Seattle to Hawaii is $1800. You can also place your vehicle in a POD alone or with other belongings. Although, Matson doesn't recommend that. You may need to make a ramp to get your car into the POD. You would need to call POD for the costs on that.

The point of preparing to move is to be organized and have all your reservations in place. This is the time to be well organized, so that everything goes smoothly. Moving is stressful enough, even if everything goes exactly right!

Chapter 5

MOVING DAY

Moving day arrives! Are you ready? Moving day is stressful. There is a lot to do, and you want it to run smoothly. Whether you have hired professional movers, gathered friends and relatives, or are loading a POD by yourself (not recommended), what can you do to make Moving Day a breeze? Three things to do on Moving Day: 1. wake up early; 2. protect floors and carpets by laying paper with tape on them to reduce dirt; 3. always tip the movers or your friends. Friends don't necessarily need money but pay it in some way.

Most times, you will be given a three-day window of when movers will come to your home, pack, and load the truck or container. (The three consecutive days are initially chosen by you.) If you have a moving company coming to your house or a POD being delivered to your house, that three-day window you want will be given to you. This is why you need to reserve a few months ahead of time. Then, twenty-four hours before or the day before, you will be given a three-hour window for movers to arrive or a POD to be dropped off. If you are having a container or POD delivered, make sure you have decided on a level, convenient place on your property for it to be placed.

DO NOT plan anything for that whole day, whether you hired a moving company, or you will have a POD delivered. Movers will take hours to wrap and load everything, even when you packed mostly everything yourself or hired a company to do it. Movers will plastic wrap boxes two to three boxes high and wrap quilted pads around all furniture with plastic wrap. Because the POD will be delivered to the port or the movers will deliver everything to a warehouse at the port or into a twenty- or forty-foot container before it is loaded onto the ship, furniture is padded and shrink-wrapped. The movers will create a custom cardboard or wooden crate for any furniture with glass on it, or furniture that is valued or expensive. For example, a cardboard crate was created to fit my piano. Also, a dresser with glass panels on the drawers was placed in a custom wooden crate. Upholstered chairs were wrapped in moving pads and then shrink-wrapped. As I mentioned, many boxes

Chapter 5

were shrink-wrapped in groups of two or three. The main point is, if you pack your boxes or bins yourself, use double-wrap, bubble wrap, and cushioned wrapping for anything breakable like glass, ceramic, and china inside the boxes. Remember that things on a ship will be moved from the waves/swells of the ocean. Boxes will be tilted from side to side, and their contents will be too. This move is more rough than a move on the Mainland. If you are packing a POD, pack it tightly and as full as possible, because contents will move.

If you are paying for extra insurance or are lucky enough to have your home owners' insurance insure the contents of your move, it is a good idea to take pictures of everything on the outside of the box and the inventory number on it. (Professional movers number everything to keep track of it.) It also isn't a bad idea to take pictures of everything you put in a box before you pack it, if possible. Why? The reason is, if a box is missing or damaged at the time of unloading, you will have proof of what is inside. Photos after delivery of everything broken is also a must. I also took pictures of the crates the movers made for my piano and antique dresser with glass. Most insurances will give you thirty to sixty days to file a claim that something is missing or broken.

On this note, it is important to keep an eye on how things are being packed and are going in a container or POD, so you are aware. Our movers were great, but all of our boxes and furniture had to be loaded on a truck. Then, it was transferred to a warehouse at the port, to wait for the ship. Then, it was transferred to a container. Then, it was placed on the ship. Once it arrived in Hilo, it was unloaded onto a truck before it was delivered to my storage and condo. Things will be missed and damaged but try to keep it to a minimum. The movers said I didn't need to be at storage to unload it, but I wanted to make sure everything was delivered and mark off which numbered boxes were there.

The following are things you should do by Moving Day:

Place all pets in boarding or bring them to a relative's or friend's house for the day. It is a stressful time for animals too, so be kind and remove them from the environment on Moving Day.

Make sure all boxes are labeled on the outside of the box, on both the top and one side, with where they go (bedroom, storage, kitchen). Label "fragile" on the top and at least one side on fragile boxes so that these can go on top of heavier boxes.

Empty all drawers in dressers, desks, tables, and cabinets. Disassemble all pieces of furniture, carts, or shelves, including bed frames. All hardware should go in a baggy and be taped strongly to the inside of a drawer or frame of the piece. Don't move anything loose. If it is loose, place it in a box.

Pack at least one of your suitcases to take on the plane. We took two each, plus carry-on. Even if you pay $25, it is cheaper than shipping

Chapter 5

it. In your suitcase, have at least seven days of clothing, and in your carry-on be sure to have all medicines, expensive jewelry and valuables, all vital documents, and the documents or moving files so they can easily be reached.

Draw a plan of where you will put furniture or boxes in your new home. This helps movers and makes you stop to think about unloading before you arrive. Remember, it can take fourteen to thirty days for things to arrive by ship.

Try to relax...until all your things get there. Depending on the time of year, it could arrive sooner than you think! That is why you bring some stuff with you when you fly over, so you have certain things that you will need.

Chapter 6

IF YOU HAVE A PET

If you have a pet, what do you need to do? Hawaii has strict laws regarding the importation of animals. Some animals that may be allowed as pets in other states, may be restricted or prohibited in Hawaii. Importing an illegal animal carries a penalty of up to three years in prison and up to $500,000 in fines. For simplification, I will concentrate on cats and dogs, the most common pets to be imported. If you are not sure about the import status of an animal, please contact the Quarantine Program at 808-832-0566.

The quarantine and admittance policy of dogs and cats changed on 8/31/2018. It is easier than it used to be, but still requires time, planning, and costs. Most importantly, go online to the Hawaii Department of Agriculture website to read recent changes and requirements. The Animal Quarantine has the mission of preventing the entry of rabies and other diseases into the state of Hawaii. Hawaii is the only rabies-free state in the nation. The website is hdoa.hawaii.gov. To prevent rabies from entering the state, the current law requires that dogs, cats, and other carnivores complete either the five-day-or-less or the 120-day Rabies Quarantine Program. The law states that dogs/cats that meet all specific pre- and post-arrival requirements may qualify for five days or less in the Direct Release Rabies Quarantine Program. What does quarantine mean? Quarantine is an isolation of your pet from other animals, to check for infections or contagious diseases. The quarantine facility is right at the Honolulu Airport. The law also requires the entire cost of the Rabies Quarantine Program be paid by the user of the quarantine facility.

First, determine if your pet should move to Hawaii. If your animal is very old, very young (less than nine weeks), chronically ill, or debilitated, you should carefully consider whether they should be shipped. Shipping is stressful for the animal and owner, and is expensive. The Department of Agriculture does not have any regulation regarding where pets fly within an aircraft on flights to Hawaii. Each airline has different policies. Please check with your airline regarding costs,

Chapter 6

requirements for flying, and placement on the aircraft. I would recommend you be on the same flight as your animal, if possible. This allows for less mishaps with the pet.

All dogs must be microchipped and neutered or spayed. The cost to be microchipped can be as low as ten dollars at the humane society, and up to seventy dollars for a private veterinarian to do it. That microchip is specific to your pet and is used to identify your pet dog, and also used to record rabies test results. So, even if your pet isn't flying, microchipping is a good source of safety for your pet. Neutering and spaying can be free at some humane societies, or for a nominal fee of forty dollars, while a private veterinarian may charge one hundred to two hundred dollars.

As I mentioned, the quarantine and admittance policy of dogs/cats to Hawaii recently changed on 8/31/2018.

If you have a pet, I believe you should keep them and work through the paperwork, because that's your responsibility as a pet owner. It is not an excuse to get rid of your pet. The quarantine and the admittance policy are actually easier now, but still require time and planning. Go to the website for the Hawaii Department of Agriculture to read recent changes and requirements. The website is" hdoa.hawaii.gov.

From hdoa.hawaii.gov, go to the Animal Quarantine Information Page. For simplification, I will concentrate on pet dogs. Again, all dogs must be microchipped AND be neutered or spayed.

The easiest and most economical way for your dog to qualify is for the five-day-or-less quarantine for the Direct Release Program. For a pet to qualify for this, there are several pre-shipment requirements that must be met. Dogs not meeting all the specific five-day-or-less program requirements will be quarantined a minimum of thirty days to a maximum of 120 days. Again, there are two main programs for dogs and cats entering Hawaii: The five-day-or-less Direct Release and the 120-day Quarantine for those dogs that do not meet the requirements for the Direct Release Program.

The Five-Day-or-Less Program

1. The pet must have been administered at least two rabies vaccines in its lifetime. The second vaccine must have been administered no less than thirty days after the first vaccine. In addition, the most recent vaccination must have been given no less than thirty days and no more than twelve months prior to arrival in Hawaii for twelve-month licensed vaccines, and no less than thirty days and no more than thirty-six months prior to arrival in Hawaii for the three-year licensed vaccines.

2. The pet should be microchipped for identification. The microchip is required to identify the pet's blood sample for rabies. On

Chapter 6

the Import Form (AQ-279), you need to record the microchip identification code.

3. A blood sample must be sent to an approved laboratory for the OIE-Fluorescent Antibody Serum (OIE-FAVN), which tests for the adequate response to the rabies vaccine. A test result > 0.5 IU/ml is required.

4. The pet must complete the required waiting period from the date the laboratory receives the blood sample before it may enter the state under the following programs:

A. Five-day-or-less quarantine requires thirty-day pre-arrival waiting period.

B. If the pre-arrival requirements are not met, then the pet will not qualify for the program and must complete a much lengthier quarantine program.

5. If your pet arrives in Hawaii before the required waiting period has elapsed, your pet will not qualify for the shorter quarantine program. Your pet must remain in quarantine until it has completed the thirty-day waiting period AFTER passing an OIE-FAVN rabies test. Your pet must also remain in quarantine until at least thirty days have passed after the most recent rabies vaccination. You will be charged $14.30 for each day in quarantine, plus $244.

6. Most airlines will require a Health Certificate completed by your veterinarian within ten to fourteen days of flying. Please consult your airline for any other requirements.

7. A Dog and Cat Import Form (AQS-279) should be completed before your flight and sent to the Animal Quarantine Station with proof of the two rabies vaccination certificates and the neuter or spay certificate. It is recommended to get this form and the certificates to them at least thirty to sixty days before the flight.

So, a little bit about costs. The 120-day quarantine program costs at least $1080 per pet. Whereas, the five-day-or-less Direct Release Program costs $244 per pet. The Direct Release Program with NO quarantine costs $185 per pet. There are no discounts on multiple pets.

The best way to get the blood tests done is to have your vet draw the blood sample in the morning on a Monday, Tuesday, or Wednesday, and have them overnight on ice the blood to the Kansas City Lab. This lab sends the test results directly to the Animal Quarantine Station and to your veterinarian. The results will also be posted on the department's website:
http://hdoa.hawaii.gov/aqs/animal-quarantine-microchip-search/

The test results are recorded by your dog's microchip number. The website is updated weekly and will also post the earliest date your

Chapter 6

pet can enter Hawaii and qualify for the five-day-or-less program based on a thirty-day waiting period.

The most expensive part of preparing your pet to fly to Hawaii, if no quarantine is needed, will be the airline ticket for your pet. It isn't unusual to cost more than your ticket.

If quarantine is needed, this will most likely be the most expensive cost, depending on the number of days.

Exemptions

The law allows exemption to quarantine for guide dogs for the blind and certified service dogs for the disabled. Guide and service dogs must still complete the pre-shipment requirements, including having a current rabies vaccine, passing an OIE-FAVN rabies blood test prior to arrival in Hawaii with a > 0.5 IU/ml, and certification.

A note about service dogs: Your service dog should be able to fly in the cabin with you. You should not have to pay for a ticket for the animal because of it being a service dog. You should still get a Health Certificate by your veterinarian within ten to fourteen days of flying. Talk to your airline for their requirements.

Chapter 7

ARRIVAL

You will receive a call, text, and/or email when your POD, container, or shipment has reached the port of its ultimate destination. You will be able to track your shipment from the time it arrives at the outgoing port to the incoming port. If you worked with a moving company, they will call you to set up a day and time for delivery. They expect shipment will leave port within three days of arrival at port. Otherwise, they may charge you for warehouse storage. A moving company will usually give you a window of three hours the day before delivery at your destination. Stay home that whole day and don't plan anything for that day.

The Journey of a Lifetime Moving to Hawaii

If a POD or container is being delivered to your Hawaii address, make sure there is a level place near your residence, to make unloading easier. Make sure you have an authorized trucking company reserved to pick up your POD or container at the port. You can call Matson or Young's Brothers to find out more, if needed. If you hire a moving company, there are a set group of movers in Hawaii who will service you. They usually unload all your belongings from the container at Hilo into a truck. Then they drive the truck to your residence or storage. They will call you when all your belongings are at the port and then call you twenty-four hours before the actual delivery with the time.

If you use professional movers, please keep track of which boxes are being delivered and which boxes are damaged or missing. You can actually be involved in the inventory check. Again, whether a moving company is unloading for you or a professional mover is, make sure you have thought about how to have all the boxes delivered to the appropriate rooms, and furniture placement in your new residence.

If everything is going in a storage unit, I would still recommend you be at the storage unit to check everything.

Shipping your car is fairly easy. The tracking number you are given by Matson or your moving company makes it possible to follow your car from port to port. Matson has a very reliable schedule. It offers seven arrivals from the West Coast to Hawaii every fourteen days. This is more

Chapter 7

than any other shipping company. You can call 1-800-4MATSON to easily obtain any information, from rate quotes, booking, billing, schedules, shipment status, and problem resolution. You must pay for the entire shipping for your car or belongings before the ship leaves port. You will be given a specific number for your car so you can track it online. It takes fourteen to thirty days for shipping, depending on how busy they are. We moved over Thanksgiving, and the service was very quick—fourteen days. When your car arrives at the port of your destination, say Hilo, they will call you and allow up to seventy-two hours to pick it up at the port. If possible, it is easier if the owner of the car and registrant picks it up. You just need your photo ID and the number given to your vehicle. Call for hours of operation and when they close for lunch to save yourself from waiting. The Port Authority takes 1.5 hours for lunch from 11:30 a.m. to 1:00 p.m. They are strict about taking their lunch time.

Once everything is unloaded and you have all your belongings and your vehicle(s), you can definitely breathe a sigh of relief because the hard part is over! Just remember, if you are claiming damage or items are missing, the insurance company should be called as soon as possible, and have them send you any forms and requirements needed to submit the claim. Usually, you have thirty to sixty days from date of delivery.

Chapter 8

WHERE WILL YOU RESIDE?

Before moving to the island, choose which part you want to live on. If you work, do you want to be close to your employer? If you have children, which school district do you want to live in? If you don't work, perhaps weather or activity sites may determine where you will live. If you surf or snorkel, you may want to be on the north or west shore.

Lastly, I will discuss renting or buying. What is the best option for you? As I mentioned in Chapter 1, spending time on a few different islands, time permitting, can give you an idea of what you like and what you can afford. Spending time in different areas of that island will also help you home in on where you will be happiest and what you can afford.

If you are newly arriving, or recently moved to Hawaii, you may want to rent an apartment, condo, or house. Some people move here with good intentions and then find that they can't afford it on their salary here, don't like it, or are too far from family. How sure are you that you will still be here in one to two years? There is nothing wrong with renting. Renting allows you to determine how much you really like the area. Other than the terms of your lease, there are no obligations.

Demand for rental properties is high. Rentals can go quickly. It is easier to find a place once you have moved on the island. You will be taken more seriously when you already live here. If you can, initially stay in a hotel apartment or short-term rental until you can actually search for yourself. The state of Hawaii ranks first in the overall cost of living and for electricity costs. The average cost for a two- to three-bedroom in Kona on the Big Island may be $2000-$2500, but it can be less in other areas. In Oahu, it is usually much more than this, depending on the area also. Many rentals will be fully or partially furnished. Rentals usually include water, sewer, or septic, and cable/DirecTV or satellite. However, most won't include electricity because of the cost. The US Energy Administration provided the information below from 2014.

Chapter 8

Hawaii and Alaska have the highest utility bills, but solar and renewable energy solutions such as wind farms and geothermal energy are constantly being upgraded for more everyday use. The Hawaii Clean Energy Initiative's goal is to switch entirely to renewable energy sources by 2045.

According to the National Light Initiative in Hawaii County, from an article in December 2018 by Amelia Josephson, Hawaii County (the Big Island) has the lowest price of renting a fair market value two-bedroom home, averaging $1271/month. In Kauai County, the cost is $1463/month, compared to $1568/month in Maui County. In Honolulu County, the fair market rental value is $1982/month. My experience is that these prices are too conservative and will be much higher.

In comparison, in 2019 the median sale prices for single-family homes on the Big Island is $368,000, Kauai $700,000, Maui $651,000, and Oahu $795,000. These prices were current at the writing of this book in early 2019. The sale prices are variable and constantly change. It is best to talk to your realtor about these.

There is no question that owning a home has its advantages. In 2018, the tax laws changed, but you can still deduct up to $10,000 of mortgage interest per year on your tax returns. When interest rates remain low, there is an advantage to buy. An issue for most new homeowners is the cash needed for a down payment. If you are buying a two-bedroom condo for $300,000, 5 percent down is $15,000, 10 percent down is $30,000, and 20 percent down is $60,000.

Of course, when you rent, you are giving money toward your landlord's retirement and not building equity. If you have a fixed rate loan, your mortgage will be similar today and ten years from now. While taxes, insurance, and home association fees/maintenance fees will likely increase, you don't have to worry about your landlord raising your rent every year or being evicted because he wants to live in the home.

As far as buying your own home, there are some terms you should be familiar with that are unique to Hawaii: Fee Simple and Leasehold.

Fee Simple is the most common type of ownership, where a buyer purchases a property outright and has the right to use the property indefinitely. The buyer pays the mortgage, property taxes, and the association fees/maintenance fees to stay in good standing. The buyer is given the title to the property and any improvements.

Leasehold is created when a landowner (Lessor) enters into an agreement called a ground lease with another person (Lessee). The Lessee rents the land from the Lessor. The buyer does not own the land. He pays ground rent. First, the buyer of the Leasehold real estate does not own the land, he only has the right to use the land for a pre-determined amount of time.

Chapter 8

Second, if the Leasehold real estate is transferred to a new owner, use of the land is limited to the remaining years covered by the original lease. At the end of the pre-determined period, the land may legally revert back to the Lessor, which is called reversion. At the end of the lease term, which is usually 55+ years, many Lessors and Lessees have agreed on a new lease, which is usually increased in cost significantly, or a Lessor may agree to sell the land to the Lessee.

The advantage of Leasehold property is that it is far less expensive to purchase than a Fee Simple property, thus making your initial investment lower and more affordable. Each year, as the lease term ticks down, the property may become less valuable and harder to sell or obtain financing on. If there are less than ten years left on the lease term, financing may not be available, and you may need to seek out a cash buyer. If you do decide to go the Leasehold route, I would recommend you seek counsel with an attorney well versed in Leasehold contracts.

Another great option, if you know you will move to Hawaii and have the money available, is to purchase a condo in Hawaii before you expect to move there. If you can financially do this, you will have use of the condo when your time is free to visit Hawaii. However, you can rent the condo at other times to earn money, or at least pay for your mortgage on it with short-term rentals. You could do the same with a home and rent it under a rental agency or VRBO, but there is more maintenance with a house, if you aren't there. A condo is easier to own because the on-site manager will have the exterior maintained with your association fees. You would only need to be concerned with maintenance of the interior. However, monthly maintenance fees can be pricey. Still, by doing it this way, when you eventually move to Hawaii, you will already have your home, and with equity built up in it.

Altogether, 48 percent of the residents of Hawaii rent rather than own. You must consider what is best for you and your family.

Chapter 9

HOME OWNERSHIP & TAX BENEFITS

Taxes—nobody likes them, and almost everyone pays them. There are some great tax breaks available if you own or are thinking of buying a home. The Homestead Tax Exemption allows homeowners to shelter or exempt part of their home's value from the property tax calculation.

In Hawaii, it is called the Real Property Tax. The county government depends on property taxes to pay for an array of services, including police and fire protection, civil defense, parks and recreation, elderly activities, solid waste program, mass transit, economic development, flood control, and animal control. It should be noted that roads, highways, and traffic lights are funded by fuel taxes, state and federal grants-in-aid, and private developers.

To calculate the amount of your tax bill, you need to find the "Net Taxable Value" of your property. This value is provided on your Real Property Tax Assessment Notice that is mailed out on March 15. Tax rates are also available on the internet, at http://www.hawaiipropertytax.com/.

The formula to calculate your taxes is as follows:

(Net Taxable Value x Tax Rate)/1000 = Taxes Due

I must admit that Hawaii does offer some real estate tax discounts of home ownership that some other states don't offer. The state of Hawaii has the lowest property tax rate in the nation. The state's average effective property tax rate is 0.27 percent to 0.291 percent, compared to an average of 1.211 percent in the nation. There are two major exemptions for homeowners in Hawaii: the Homeowner's Exemption and the Disability Exemption.

The Homeowner's Exemption is deducted from the assessed value of your property to help reduce the net taxable value of the property. The basic home exemption is $40,000, for homeowners sixty to sixty-nine years of age it is $80,000, and for homeowners seventy years and older, it is $100,000. An additional exemption of 20 percent of the assessed value of the property not to exceed $80,000 was enacted in

Chapter 9

2005. You are entitled to the home exemption if you own and occupy the property as your primary residence and file or intend to file your resident Hawaii state income tax return or apply for a waiver of this requirement. You must file a claim, Form 19-71, for the home exemption on or before December 31 for the first half-payment, and June 30 for the second half-payment.

The Disability Exemption is deducted from the assessed value of your property to help reduce the net taxable value of the property. If you have Hansen's Disease (Leprosy), have impaired sight or hearing, or are totally disabled, you may file a disability claim, for $50,000 Real Property Tax exemption. This claim is in addition to the regular home exemption and must be filed on the same parcel. Certification of disability must be filed on Form 19-75(A).

If you are a totally disabled veteran, your principle home is exempt from property taxes except for the minimum tax amount. You must submit Form 19-73.

Parcels of Real Property Tax, including those that qualify for a home exemption, are subject to a minimum tax of $200 with the exception: If the property owner receives a home exemption or a totally disabled exemption, resulting in the minimum tax and the assessed value of the improvements:

$50,001 to $75,000, minimum tax is $150.

$25,001 to $50,000, minimum tax is $100.

Up to $25,000, minimum tax is $50.

If your mortgage is in both your and your spouse's or partner's name, you each can file for exemptions as is allowed.

Whereas Hawaii has the highest effective income tax of all fifty states, Hawaii's state and local sales tax is lower than some other states.

Chapter 10

CHANGE OF ADDRESS

What are all the businesses and who are the people that need to know you have a change of address, email address, and phone number? The first change you should make is to notify the post office at least thirty days prior to the move. This can be done by computer now at: http://www.usps.com/. It will cost one dollar, but it is worth the expense to have your mail forwarded to your new address. This allows forwarding of First-Class Mail for up to twelve months and periodicals up to sixty days. There is permanent and temporary, if you plan to move back in twelve months.

Create a checklist of places you should notify when you change addresses.

Moving Company, POD, or Matson.

Place of Employment—the one you are leaving and the one you are starting. You will probably have paychecks or retirement, or benefit information that your employer needs to send you.

Financial Institutions, Attorneys, Accountants, Financial Planners, and Banks, and all bank accounts, investments, stocks, auto loans, mortgage companies of other property owned, or time shares. Some will want it in writing or emailed.

Credit Card Companies—some of mine wanted to know only after I moved, or on the day of moving. You don't want to be late on credit card payments because of your move. There may be a penalty or a late charge.

Utilities—Cable, Internet, TV, Phone Providers, Electricity, Gas, Water, Trash. These services will also want to know the date you want your services turned off under your name. You don't want to be moving in the dark or without water. These providers also need your address, email, and phone number to send you your last bill, or perhaps a credit. You also want to make sure your trash is picked up upon moving out, and not left at your home after the fact. They will want to know your last pick-up date, and if you want your trash bins collected.

Chapter 10

Doctor, Dentist, Optometrist—any medical professional you see regularly. You may want to secure a copy of your medical records to take with you.

Health, Vision, and Dental Insurance, Prescription Carrier—when moving out of state, you will probably need to change your carrier or change to one your new employer is offering. If you are retired, call Social Security to give them your new address, phone, and email. You also may need to change your bank for direct deposit of your check. The contact information for Social Security is 1-800-772-1213. TTY is 1-800-325-0778. Website is http://www.socialsecurity.gov/. For Medicare, phone is 1-800-medicare. TTY is 1-877-486-2048. Website is http://www.medicare.gov/. If your previous employer is paying for your health insurance after retirement, call your benefit contact of your employer. Rates will likely be different in different states, and the carrier may be too. Also find out about your prescription carrier.

Life Insurance Companies.

Auto Insurance—most auto insurance carriers have agents in other states to help you insure your vehicle and get Proof of Insurance and a new ID card. This is important in Hawaii, because to get your vehicle registered and pass the Safety Inspection, it is mandatory to have a hard copy of your vehicle coverage under your Hawaii auto insurance.

You can't pass the Safety Inspection or get your vehicle registered in Hawaii without it.

Rental or Home Insurance—also you need to stop your coverage on your insurance for your previous home or rental AFTER you move, though it can be as early as the next day. You need to obtain new coverage for your residence in Hawaii, as well.

Schools and Colleges—provide your forwarding address for the college you just attended or your child's school. Also get a copy of your child's immunization record from school or their pediatrician.

Pet's Veterinarian—any records will be helpful, including your pet's health insurance, if you have it.

Organizations that you are members of, whether for work, charities, licenses, or churches.

Circulation Departments—magazines, newspapers, catalogues. Stop newspaper delivery and give them your new address for credits.

Anyone who may need to send final bills or information about their professional services to your new state.

Frequent Flier Programs, Hotel Honors Programs, Rental Car Rewards, AAA.

Friends and Family.

Chapter 11

DRIVER'S LICENSE & REGISTRATION

Accept that you will be spending time at the DMV if you own a vehicle or want to drive a vehicle in Hawaii. Every state has different requirements on obtaining a driver's license as a resident of that state, as well as on obtaining a registration or safety inspection of your vehicle, too. Once you have moved, you can check out the nearest Department of Motor Vehicles online and find answers to some of your questions. You will find out how to transfer an out-of-state license to one in Hawaii. It depends on what state you are moving from. As an example, having a valid California driver's license, plus some other proof of my new address and residency in Hawaii, I was able to transfer it without too much difficulty.

Obtaining a Hawaii Driver's License

Any expired out-of-state license is not transferable and requires the successful completion of both written and road tests.

You may drive in Hawaii with a valid driver's license issued by any state if you are eighteen years of age or older. Upon moving to Hawaii, you have thirty to sixty days to transfer your out-of-state license to a Hawaii driver's license. You must comply with the following requirements before the expiration of your out-of-state license:

- Provide Proof of Legal Presence

- Provide Proof of Principle Residence

- Complete a Driver's License Application that is available at any driver licensing office in Hawaii

- Be eighteen years of age or older

- Present Proof of Social Security Number with an original Social Security Card that has the printed name of the applicant, or a Medicare Card with the name and Social Security number on it

- A Military ID Card or an original DD-214 are also acceptable for the previous requirement

- Surrender your valid plastic driver's license that was issued by the other state

Chapter 11

- Complete and Pass Eye Screening Test

- Have a clear driving record on the National Driver Registry

Proof of Legal Presence is proof that a person is either a US citizen or is legally authorized to be in the US. Proof documents to verify legal presence include birth certificates and passports.

Two forms of documentation are required for Proof of Principle Residence. Principle Residence is defined as the location where a person currently resides, even if the residence is temporary. Any two of the following documents:

- A current and valid Hawaii State ID card or Hawaii driver's license

- Vehicle registration or title

- Utility bill with the applicant's name and address, not more than two months old

- Checking or Savings statement, not more than two months old

- Payroll check issued by employer within last two months

- Current Mortgage Account or Proof of Home Ownership

- Residential rental or time share contract for six months

- US Income Tax Return or Hawaii Income Tax Return, W-2 or 1099 SSA benefits from the previous year

- Receipt for Personal Property Taxes to a county in the state of Hawaii within the past year

- Medical Card issued with principle residence printed on it
- Current Property Tax Assessment Bill or Statement
- See List of Acceptable Documents Form.

Vehicle Registration and Safety Inspection

After your vehicle arrives here and you pick it up at the port, it's time to get it registered. You have thirty to sixty days to get the Safety Inspection and Registration. The following is what is required for Vehicle Registration:

- For new vehicles entering the state with model years from the past year, current year, and next year, you need to complete State of Hawaii Form G-27
- Original Certificate of Title (if available)
- Original Certificate of Registration (from the state you are leaving)
- Current or Temporary Safety Inspection
- Bill of Lading (Shipping Document)
- State of Hawaii Tax Clearance

To get your vehicle inspected, you need to visit an authorized state inspection station (make an appointment). You will need your current registration from the state you moved from. You will need to bring in your ORIGINAL Hawaii car insurance ID card, or have it emailed or

Chapter 11

faxed from the insurance company. After review of the above forms, the safety check inspector will check:

- Steering
- Alignment
- Suspension
- Tires
- Wheels and Rims
- Exhaust System
- Fuel and Intake Systems
- Brakes, including parking brake
- Lamps
- Horn
- Window Tint
- Windshield and Wipers
- Rearview Mirrors
- Door Latches
- Seats and Seatbelts
- Fenders
- Bumpers
- Floor
- Speedometer and Odometer
- Registration

The Journey of a Lifetime Moving to Hawaii

If your vehicle is from out of state, it WILL FAIL the inspection due to out-of-state registration (this failure is what triggers the state of Hawaii to be able to give you a new Hawaii Registration). After the inspector fails your vehicle for out-of-state registration, you will be required to pay for the inspection at that time, approximately twenty dollars. The safety inspector will give you paperwork and you will need to take that to your local DMV in Hawaii, where they will give you a new Hawaii Registration. Then, you need to bring that new registration back to the safety inspector, and your safety inspector will put the NEW Safety Sticker on your license plate. For all of this, I recommend you get your Hawaii license plate on before the inspection sticker. Also, save a day to complete this running around.

The Bill of Lading is a large sticker that will be given to you at the port of pick-up for your car. This, you need to give to the DMV for registration.

You will need to complete the State of Hawaii Department of Taxation's Motor Vehicle Use Tax Certificate that you get from the Department of Taxation. On the Big Island, Kona Office is in the State Office Building at 82-6130 Mamalahoa Hwy, Captain Cook 96704, phone 808-974-6321, and Hilo Office is at 75 Aupuni St, Suite 101, Hilo 96720, phone 808-974-6321. For me, no use tax was due because it was shipped over with my household goods.

Chapter 11

Then, for registration, I also needed to take my car and have it weighed at a Certified Weigh Station. For this, I went to Kona and paid $36.46.

Certified Weigh Station locations:

West Hawaii Concrete 808-329-3561
74-4925 Queen Kaahumanu Hwy, Kailua-Kona 96740

West Hawaii Concrete 808-885-7307
67-2399 Mamaloha Hwy, Kamuela 96743

Hawaiian Homelands Dept. 808-887-6053
Call for appt. here
64-756 Mamalahoa Hwy, Kamuela 96743

Puna Rock Co. 808-966-7625
16-669 Milo St, Keaau 96749

James Glover, LTD 808-443-5384
890 Leilani St, Hilo 96720

So, there is a lot of running around to get your vehicle registered and get your Hawaii license plates from the DMV.

County of Hawaii DMV locations:

Kona-Hawaii Civic Center

74-5044 Ane Keohokalole Hwy, Bldg C

Kona 96740

Phone 808-323-4818

Hours M-F 8 a.m. to 4 p.m.

Pahoa

15-2615 Keaau-Pahoa Rd, Pahoa 96778

Phone 808-965-2721

Hours M-F 8 a.m. to 3:30 p.m.

Waimea

65-1158 Mamalahoa Hwy, Suite 1A

Kamuela 96743

Phone 808-881-3488

Hours M-F 8 a.m. to 4 p.m.

Hilo

101 Pauahi St,

Hilo 96720

Phone 808-961-8351

Chapter 11

Hours M-F 8 a.m. to 4 p.m.

If you need handicapped plates or placards after you get your license plate, go to the Office of Aging. In Kona, it is in the same building as the DMV. Pick up the Disability Parking Application and have your Hawaii-licensed doctor complete it. Then, return the form to the Office of Aging to get a placard and turn in your plates at the DMV to get handicapped plates.

Chapter 12

ENJOY!

You have earned it! Enjoy Hawaii. Once you get settled in Hawaii and have a home or apartment, a state ID or Hawaii driver's license, any vehicle inspected, insured and registered, utilities in your name, established employment or retirement, and find a health insurance so you can see a dentist and a doctor, you can establish your church, volunteer activities, clubs and activity groups, if desired.

With any time left over, get to know the area where you live. Are you happy there? Is it financially acceptable? Have you made friends in the area? Is shopping, car maintenance and banking accessible? Is your doctor close by? How far is your church? How far are the schools? Is it affordable for you?

If you can answer "YES" to most of these questions, sit back and enjoy. Find the things you like to do in the area. Hawaii of course is great for hiking, cycling, rock climbing, scuba, surfing, snorkeling and swimming. Most of these will be within an hour of where you live. Driving to the mountains and ranches, horseback riding, farming, and getting fresh produce should all be accessible.

One advantage of living in Hawaii full-time is you qualify for the "kama'aina" discount. You need to have proof of residency with a Hawaii driver's license or a Hawaii state ID card. Go to http://www.hidot.hawaii.gov/ for the requirements to obtain an ID card and where to get one. The kama'aina discount can include activities, tours, hotels, some restaurants and stores. Ask the place of service if the discount is offered because it isn't necessarily advertised.

Hawaii is great for volunteering. Whether it be helping the poor, homeless, your parish/church, the environment, humane society, hospitals, seniors, marine life, flora or fauna. The island is a limited population, so it isn't hard to get involved. Give back to the community that you are supporting and is supporting you.

Playing devil's advocate, if you have school-age children, you may consider private schools. More than 17 percent of Hawaii's children

Chapter 12

attend private schools. Even though schools have improved in Hawaii, many schools have students who score below average on standardized tests. The quality in Hawaii's schools does vary greatly.

The cost of living is the highest of all fifty states. Coming from New York and then California, I wasn't too shocked. However, when you compare the cost of living to your current city (like San Francisco), it may not seem too bad. Housing will be your biggest cost. The Big Island has such variety in home prices, though, depending on the location. If you are willing to do what it takes, live in a cheaper area or live in a more expensive area and pick up a second job to pay the price.

Can you live without four seasons? Hawaii has two seasons, mainly rainy from November to April, and dry from May to October. Yet, this varies on the Big Island too. Kona is usually sunny and warm. Even in the rainy season, it is mostly sunny. However, Hawi and Hilo are different.

Also, think about whether you mind that you will be separated from family and friends. You can always fly to the Mainland, and prices vary for that as well.

If you decide, after thinking about all these things, that you are not willing or ready to make certain sacrifices, that is okay. Keep in mind that this is a decision you might want to revisit every year or two. A change in life circumstances may also change the sacrifices you need to make.

Despite all the challenges, there is no place I would rather be living right now. For me, the sacrifices that I have had to make are worth it, and every day I encounter people from all walks of life who seem to feel the same way.

If this is what you eventually decide, Aloha! Welcome to your new life in Hawaii!

References

Radley, D. C., McCarthy, D., & Hayes, S. L. (2018, May 3). *2018 Scorecard on State Health System Perfomance* (1-14). New York, N.Y.: The Common Wealth Fund.

"Quick Facts :Hawaii County and State of Hawaii" Retrieved from www.hawaiicounty.gov

"Quick Facts: Hawaii County," US Census Bureau Retrieved from www.census.gov/quickfacts/hawaiicounty

"Quick Facts: Honolulu County," U.S. Census Bureau Retrieved from www.census.gov/quickfacts/honolulucounty

"Quick Facts: Honolulu County," U.S. Census Bureau Retrieved from www.uscenus.com

"Quick Facts: Kauai County," US Census Bureau Retrieved from www.census.gov/quickfacts/kauaicounty

"Quick Facts: Maui County," US Census Bureau, Retrieved from www.census.gov/quickfacts/mauicounty

About the Author

Do you dream of a life with warm breezes, neighbors who live "aloha", and beaches that are in your backyard? I am one of the fortunate few who as an East Coast transplant, achieved not only my dream of becoming a physician, but also of living in Hawaii, both" journeys of a lifetime." I chose to write this book because you may just be curious or a travel adventurer or" even someone who wants to make Hawaii their home. For all of these reasons, this is the book for you! It will help you plan, save for and organize your move to Hawaii, as well as, what to do after you get there.

My credibility extends back to my first visit to Oahu, Maui and Hawaii in 1984, after graduating with my medical degree from New York College of Osteopathic Medicine. It reaches back to when I obtained my medical license in Hawaii because I spent time on Lanai in 1988, as a Family Medicine Physician during my residency. During the time that I worked" as a physician in my office in Rochester, New York for 16 years, I was fortunate to take many vacations to Kauai, Oahu, Maui, Molokai, Lanai and Hawaii. As fate would have it, I developed some serious medical issues and by 2004, I could no longer work as a physician. After 2004, I worked on personal development and had no reason to delay my plans to move to Hawaii. In 2004-2006, I traveled to and stayed" for extended periods of time in Oahu, Maui and Hawaii to see what life was truly like on these islands. In 2006, I moved from New York State to California and Hawaii (part-time) and purchased a condo in Kona. Ultimately in November, 2018, I moved to Kona full-time. I realized, firsthand, just how different moving from the Mainland to Hawaii was as compared to a move on the Mainland. There are few contemporary books written on moving to Hawaii and once there, what you need to do to set up "living." This book was written with much aloha and welcomes all those who dream and live the dream, "The Journey of A Lifetime."

www.ingramcontent.com/pod-product-compliance
Lightning Source LLC
Chambersburg PA
CBHW070436010526
44118CB00014B/2074